Growing Up AROUND THE WORLD

Growing Up in Japan

Other titles in the *Growing Up Around the World* series include:

Growing Up in Brazil
Growing Up in Canada
Growing Up in China
Growing Up in Germany
Growing Up in India
Growing Up in Iran
Growing Up in Italy
Growing Up in Mexico
Growing Up in Russia

Growing Up
AROUND THE WORLD

Growing Up in Japan

Andrea C. Nakaya

ReferencePoint Press®

San Diego, CA

ReferencePoint Press®

Printed in the United States

For more information, contact:
ReferencePoint Press, Inc.
PO Box 27779
San Diego, CA 92198
www.ReferencePointPress.com

LIBRARY OF CONGRESS CATALOGING-IN-PUBLICATION DATA

Name: Nakaya, Andrea C., 1976– author.
Title: Growing Up in Japan/by Andrea C. Nakaya.
Description: San Diego, CA: ReferencePoint Press, 2018. | Series: Growing Up Around the World series | Includes bibliographical references and index.
Identifiers: LCCN 2016059331 (print) | LCCN 2017000121 (ebook) | ISBN 9781682822197 (hardback) | ISBN 9781682822203 (eBook)
Subjects: LCSH: Japan—Social life and customs—Juvenile literature. | Adolescence—Japan—Juvenile literature. | Children—Japan—Juvenile literature. | Families—Japan—Juvenile literature. | Education—Japan—Juvenile literature.
Classification: LCC DS822.5 .N364 2018 (print) | LCC DS822.5 (ebook) | DDC 952--dc23
LC record available at https://lccn.loc.gov/2016059331

CONTENTS

JAPAN AT A GLANCE

Official Name
Japan

Size
145,914 square miles
(377,916 sq. km)

Total Population
126,702,133

Youth Population
0–14 years: 16,436,651
(12.97% of total)
15–24 years: 12,250,157
(9.67% of total)

Ethnic Groups
Japanese: 98.5%
Korean: 0.5%
Chinese: 0.4%
Other: 0.6%

Religion
Shintoism: 79.2%
Buddhism: 66.8%
Christianity: 1.5%
Other: 7.1%

Total is greater than 100% because many people practice both Buddhism and Shintoism

Capital
Tokyo

Type of Government
Parliamentary constitutional monarchy

Language
Japanese

Currency
Yen

Industries
Motor vehicles, electronic equipment, machine tools, steel and nonferrous metals, ships, chemicals, textiles, processed foods

Internet Users
118.4 million (93.3% of the population)

CHAPTER ONE

Japan and Its People

Japan has a unique culture, unlike any other in the world. Most historians believe that its first inhabitants arrived in prehistoric times. Over the thousands of years that have followed, the country has developed its own distinctive way of life. Japanese people have many things in common with other societies, but they also do things in a way that is uniquely their own.

Even Japan's geography is unique. Located in the Pacific Ocean, off the east coast of Asia, Japan consists of more than six thousand islands. These islands, which are actually the tops of a chain of volcanic mountains that rise above the ocean, are mostly uninhabited. The land area of Japan is slightly smaller than that of California. The four major islands, where the majority of Japan's population lives, are Hokkaido, Honshu, Shikoku, and Kyushu. Honshu is the largest of the four, and it contains the Kanto Plain, which is the biggest area of flat land in Japan and the location of its capital city, Tokyo.

Geography

Most of Japan is mountainous and covered with forest. Yabe Mitsuo, a former coordinator in Japan's Forestry Agency, explains that the country is unusual among industrialized nations in having so much forest. "Anyone flying over Japan is surprised at how much forest there is," he says. "Japan is heavily industrialized and one of the most densely populated countries in the world, but even so, 67% of the land is covered in forest."[1] Mitsuo explains that one of the main reasons Japan has so much forest instead of developed land is that it has steep mountain slopes that make land development difficult. In addition, the country has a humid, temperate climate where trees and plants grow well. Japan's many mountain ranges contain a number of active and dormant volcanoes, including Mount Fuji, which is a dormant volcano and the tallest mountain in Japan.

Known as a megacity, Tokyo is the country's capital and home to about 38 million people. Mount Fuji, the tallest mountain in Japan, looms in the distance.

Japan is located along the Ring of Fire, a 25,000-mile (40,234-km) horseshoe-shaped area that partially encircles a large region of the Pacific Ocean. Along this ring earthquakes and volcanic eruptions regularly occur. Because Japan has more earthquakes than most other places in the world, all Japanese young people learn to be prepared for them. For example, at schools they participate in regular earthquake drills, where they learn to get under their desks and hold on to the legs of the desk until the earthquake stops. Each student also has a special fireproof hood to wear in case an earthquake sparks a fire, which sometimes does occur. Young people even spend time in earthquake simulation machines so that they can become familiar with the feeling of being in an earthquake. Ben Cowles was working as an English teacher at a Japanese middle school

2011 Earthquake

While Japan strives to be well prepared for earthquakes, some of the earthquakes that have struck the country have been so severe that despite this state of readiness, there has been extensive and long-lasting damage. For example, in 2011 the country experienced one of its strongest earthquakes. A 9.1 magnitude earthquake struck off the northeast coast of Honshu island. Thousands of people were killed in the quake and the 30-foot-high (9-m) tsunami wave that it generated. In addition, it caused a partial meltdown at the Fukushima Daiichi nuclear power plant. Hiroyasu Haga lived in Otsuchi, a city devastated by the quake. "This town was built over hundreds and hundreds of years, but in . . . just 10 or 15 minutes it was completely destroyed," he says. "I saw people lose their lives just in front me. How do you recover from that?" According to a 2016 article in *USA Today*, years later recovery from the 2011 quake was ongoing, with more than fifty thousand people still living in temporary homes. *USA Today* also reported that of the approximately six hundred seawalls and levees that were planned along the coast, only about seventy had been completed.

Quoted in Kirk Spitzer, "5 Years Later, Japan Still Struggles to Recover from Tsunami Disaster," *USA Today*, March 10, 2016. www.usatoday.com.

near Tokyo during a major earthquake in 2011. He says that the shaking at his school was significant but observes that students were well prepared for what happened. While he found himself shaking uncontrollably, even after the quake had stopped, he says, "I was surprised at how calm and quiet they were." After the quake, he left school and says that he found the same attitude of calm elsewhere. Overall, he says, "life carried on as normal. I tried to gauge the faces of everyone. Were they scared? Apparently not."[2]

Climate and Seasons

From north to south Japan extends for about 1,800 miles (2,897 km). Because of this, its climate varies significantly from one place to another. In general, though, Japanese people live in a climate that is relatively humid and receives a lot of rain. For instance, Tokyo receives an average of about 60 inches (152 cm) of rain per year. Japan also has four distinct seasons: spring, summer, autumn, and winter. In the northern part of the country, winters can be long, with a lot of snowfall; however, the southern portion of the country usually has short, mild winters and long, hot summers. Japan also experiences typhoons in the summer. Called hurricanes when they occur in the Atlantic Ocean, these storms cause torrential rainfall, strong winds, and damaging high tides. For instance, in 2016 Typhoon Lionrock struck northern Japan, causing severe flooding and killing more than twenty people. When there is a typhoon warning, school is canceled, or if children are already at school, they are sent home.

Despite the extreme weather that sometimes occurs, the Japanese people embrace and celebrate their country's seasons. In the spring, for example, young people enjoy cherry blossom festivals, or hanami (literally, "viewing flowers") with friends and family. During these festivals young and old picnic outside and enjoy the cherry blossoms that only flower for a couple of weeks every year. Some hanami-viewing parties are tranquil, but others are very lively. For example, Tokyo's Yoyogi Park is known for its party-like atmosphere and is a favorite spot for teens at this time of year. Large numbers of them

People picnic under the cherry blossoms in Tokyo's Yoyogi Park. The springtime hanami celebration is among the most popular festivals in Japan.

congregate under the cherry blossoms at the park, where they eat, drink, and are entertained by music, street performers, and markets. Other seasonal pastimes that are very popular among Japanese young people are skiing and snowboarding. The country has numerous ski resorts, and many people live within a few hours of one, so it is common to go on weekend ski trips.

Cities

Japan is a comparatively small but densely populated nation. Its more than 126 million people live in urban areas, in relatively close proximity to each other. While the United States has approximately 35 people per square kilometer of land, Japan has about 348.

About 38 million of Japan's citizens live in Tokyo, the country's capital and its largest city. Tokyo is so big that it is commonly referred to as a megacity, and visitors are often amazed at just how many people live there. For example, one traveler talks about visiting the famous pedestrian crossing outside Shibuya train station in Tokyo. At this intersection, all the traffic lights turn red at the same time, and pedestrians surge into the street from every direction. It is one of the world's busiest pedestrian crossings, with hundreds and sometimes even thousands of people crossing every time the traffic lights turn red. The traveler comments, "It's like walking into an awesome movie battle scene and coming out alive."[3]

Even though they are packed full of people, cities in Japan are known for their cleanliness, and visitors often remark on just how clean Japan is compared to other countries. As another traveler notes, "Tokyo is so clean to the point where it almost looks brand new. Not one scrap of rubbish is strewn on the pathways or dropped as litter; no large bin bags are left festering for collection; the 'five-second' rule of eating something dropped on the floor could turn into the 'five-minute' rule; and no graffiti can be found covering an old wall or alleyway."[4]

Public Transportation

Most of the millions of people living in Tokyo and other Japanese cities rely on public transportation rather than driving their own cars. Young people in particular rarely have cars of their own in the cities or in any part of Japan. The main reason for this is that young people are not even allowed to obtain a driver's license until they are at least eighteen years old. Further, the process of studying for, and passing, the driver's license test is notoriously difficult and expensive, which means that many young people do not even attempt it. Japanese youth Kei Keiko knows many people who have failed or quit because the process was so difficult. She says, "TO PASS THE MLT [Ministry of Land and Transport] EXAMS AND GET THE DRIVING LICENSE IS LIKE WINNING A LOTTERY TICKET!!"[5]

> "TO PASS THE MLT [Ministry of Land and Transport] EXAMS AND GET THE DRIVING LICENSE IS LIKE WINNING A LOTTERY TICKET!!"[5]
>
> —Kei Keiko, Japanese youth

Ainu descendants

The Ainu are the indigenous people of Japan's northern island of Hokkaido. This small ethnic minority struggles to survive in modern Japan. Its decline began in the fifteenth century, when the Ainu were crowded out by Japanese settlers and weakened by the infectious diseases these settlers brought with them. In the late 1800s the government caused further destruction of the Ainu culture by banning the Ainu language, putting Ainu children in Japanese schools, and giving them Japanese names. Overall, the Ainu were marginalized and poorly treated for many years. It was not until 2008 that the Japanese government finally recognized them as indigenous to Japan, with a distinctive language and culture of their own. Despite this recognition, the Ainu have had difficulty recovering from so many years of mistreatment. Shunwa Honda, a scholar who studies Japan's indigenous ethnic groups, says, "Twice the number of Ainu are on social welfare compared to the majority Japanese population. Education levels are much lower and they have economic restraints." It is estimated that fewer than twenty-four thousand Ainu are left in Japan, and according to the Endangered Languages Project, their native language is critically endangered, with only two native speakers still living.

Quoted in Dean Irvine, "Japan's Hidden People: Ainu Try to Keep Ancient Traditions Alive," CNN, February 9, 2015. www.cnn.com.

Even after obtaining a license, the daily costs of owning a car, such as insurance and parking fees, are so high that they are unaffordable for most young people in Japan.

Instead, young people usually ride bikes or travel by bus or train. The Shinkansen, or bullet train, is one of the most well-known types of public transportation in Japan. These trains travel at speeds up to 200 miles per hour (322 kph) and usually run on time, down to the second. While the bullet train travels extremely fast, it is also a very smooth ride. Blogger Mary Moriarty writes about riding the bullet train when she was in Japan: "When you ride on the train [it's] similar to the experience of riding in an airplane—you know you're going fast because you are passing things at great speeds, but it doesn't feel fast—it just feels like you are riding on a train."[6] She says that she traveled from the Shinkansen station in Nishi Akashi to Tokyo in only two and a half hours, while a bus ride would have taken eight hours.

Life in the Country

While the majority of Japan's population lives in its cities and urban areas, some young people grow up in the countryside, where life is quite different. In contrast to urban areas, where they are always surrounded by crowds of strangers, young people living in the country say that they are surrounded by people they know. They are also surrounded by nature, in contrast to Japan's cities, where nature has been replaced by roads and buildings. One thing that many young people do not like about the countryside, however, is its lack of technology and entertainment choices. Japan's urban areas offer young people easy access to a huge variety of shopping, entertainment, and technology. In contrast, a small country town may have no high-speed Internet and only one grocery store.

Whether they live in the country or the city, most Japanese young people grow up in an environment that is extremely safe compared to many other countries. When it comes to crime, Japan is one of the safest countries in the world, with very low crime rates. For instance, a 2016 *New York Times* report compared crime rates in Japan and the United States. According to the report, Japan's homicide rate in 2013 was only 0.3 per 100,000 people, compared to 3.8 in the United States. That same year, Japan experienced 13 gun murders compared to 8,454 in the United States. Becky Osawa is from Canada but has been living in Japan teaching English since 2010. She says, "There's no such thing as 100% crime free, but Japan is (seriously) one of the safest places in the world. It's not at all uncommon to see elementary school kids going out and about on their own to the grocery store or on public transit."[7]

> "There's no such thing as 100% crime free, but Japan is (seriously) one of the safest places in the world."[7]
>
> —Becky Osawa, who teaches English in Japan

A Changing Population

While it currently remains one of the most populous countries in the world, Japan is experiencing significant changes to its population. Firstly, it has a very low birth rate. Large numbers of Japanese people are choosing not to have any children or to only have one child, and the result is that Japan's population is shrinking. The Statistics Bureau of Japan reports that between 2010 and 2015, the population declined by almost 1 million people, a decrease of about 15 percent per year. In addition to shrinking, Japan's population is aging. The proportion of old people is far greater than that of young people, and this difference is becoming more pronounced every year. At present, only about 13 percent of Japan's population is age fourteen and under. Fifteen- to twenty-four-year-olds make up only about 10 percent more of the population. In contrast, those sixty-five and older make up close to 30 percent. An official from Japan's Ministry of Internal Affairs stresses, "The ratio of people aged 65 or older is the highest ever recorded."[8] In addition to having the highest ratio of elderly people in its own history, Japan is also believed to have the highest ratio in the world. That ratio is expected to increase in the future. The Pew Research Center projects that the median age in Japan will increase from forty-five in 2010 to fifty-three in 2050.

Japanese men and women over the age of sixty-five make up nearly 30 percent of the country's population, a proportion that is far greater than that of young people.

The country's relatively low immigration rate does not help the situation. Some countries gain young people through immigration. However, Japan integrates only a very small number of new immigrants every year and remains peopled primarily by ethnic Japanese. According to *The CIA World Factbook*, Japan's population is 98.5 percent Japanese. The next most common ethnic groups are Korean and Chinese, which each constitutes less than half a percent of the population.

Young people worry that the country's low immigration and birth rates, combined with its aging population, will complicate their futures. When youth enter the workforce, their taxes and contributions to social security help support elderly retirees. But as the number of youth entering the workforce shrinks and the elderly population grows, Japan's youth fear that they might be working harder and paying more taxes to care for their elders. To combat the threats of an aging and shrinking population, Japan's government has announced that it plans to take various actions to encourage people to have more children, such as making it easier for working mothers to find day care for their children. However, many young people worry that the situation has become so severe that these actions will not be enough.

> "I can't count the number of trains I've been on that have been delayed because of suicides—and that in itself is a bit disturbing."[9]
>
> —Grace Buchele Mineta, a writer who has lived in Tokyo

Suicide

Concerns about the shrinking youth population are compounded by the high suicide rate among teens and young adults. Suicide is a leading cause of death in Japan, and the country has one of the highest rates of suicide in the world. The *Japan Times* reports that in 2014, suicide was the leading cause of death for people aged fifteen to thirty-nine, and it accounted for half of all deaths among those ages twenty to twenty-nine. A common way that young people commit suicide is by jumping in front of one of Japan's many trains. Writer Grace Buchele Mineta spent some time living in Tokyo, and she comments, "I can't count the number of trains I've been on that have been delayed because of suicides—and that in itself is a bit disturbing. Let me repeat that: *It's happened so often, I've stopped counting*."[9]

Experts believe that there are a number of possible reasons for Japan's high suicide rate. One theory is that many people cannot deal with the strong pressure that Japanese society puts on them to work hard and fit in with others at work or school. For example, Japanese students face strong expectations to do well on exams and to fit in with their peers. Those who do not are often bullied. Government researchers analyzed the country's suicide data and found evidence that this pressure causes suicide; they found that Japanese youth are most likely to kill themselves on September 1, the day that most students return to school after summer vacation. Another possible reason for high suicide rates is that suicide seems to be more culturally acceptable in Japan. While many Western cultures believe that suicide is wrong, the same stigma does not exist in Japan. In fact, there is a strong cultural tradition of honorable suicide. For instance, defeated Samurai warriors traditionally committed suicide in order to preserve their honor. Researchers believe that many teens and young adults see suicide as an honorable way to deal with failure or defeat.

Government

Getting young people to change their attitudes toward fitting into the larger group, suicide, and other concerns—both social and political—can be challenging. Japan has a democratic government, and youth are allowed take part in the political process when they reach eighteen and are eligible to vote. However, even after they turn eighteen most youth in Japan have only limited involvement in the political process. Some people believe this is due to the fact that youth generally receive little political education in school. (Japanese law prohibits schools from supporting or opposing any particular political party, so many teachers simply avoid the subject.) In addition, until 2016 young people were not even permitted to vote until the age of twenty. In recent years there have been some signs of greater political awareness among Japan's young people. For example, in 2015 thousands of youth publicly protested against a bill that would allow Japan to send troops overseas for the first time since World War II. However, many Japanese young people do not get involved in politics. Many insist that politics is pointless for them, arguing that their votes will not make a difference because they are vastly outnumbered by their elders. Overall, says college student Kosuke Furui, "Young people feel terribly powerless."[10]

Voter participation is an important part of Japan's government, though. The country has a democratic government with three branches: legislative, executive, and judicial. The government's legislative body, called the Diet, selects a prime minister, who serves as head of the government. In addition, Japan has an emperor; however, his role is largely symbolic. Emperor Akihito ascended to the throne in 1990 and is the only monarch in the world with the title of emperor. While the prime minister and the Diet oversee matters of national importance, at the local level Japan is divided into forty-seven prefectures, each with its own governor and officials.

> "Young people feel terribly powerless."[10]
>
> —Kosuke Furui, a college student

One unusual part of Japan's constitution is a section that renounces war as a national policy. This position was adopted following the country's traumatic defeat in World War II, when the United States dropped two atomic bombs on the Japanese cities of Hiroshima and Nagasaki. The cities were destroyed, and tens of thousands of people died instantly, with thousands more dying later from radiation exposure. Japan was forced to surrender. In order to prevent such a terrible experience from ever happening again, Japan adopted a constitution that states it can only maintain a defensive army and cannot become a military threat again. Although Japan's defeat in World War II was devastating, the country did not remain down for long. Following the war, it quickly recovered by directing its energy into its economy. By the 1980s Japan had become one of the world's largest economic powers, and it continues to play an important role in world affairs. Yet as its constitution shows, while Japan moves ahead, it also remembers its past. Throughout its long history, Japanese society has continued to evolve, but at the same time it has preserved many customs and traditions, and the result is a rich and unique culture.

CHAPTER TWO

Home and Family

Lucky Drops is a house in downtown Tokyo. Like most Japanese houses it has a kitchen, a bathroom, and a sleeping area. It even has three levels. What makes the house unusual is that it is only 10 feet (3 m) wide at its widest point. Architect Yasuhiro Yamashita explains that he only had a tiny piece of land to build on and had to be very creative to fit a house onto it. However, he believes that the result is beautiful. According to Yamashita, the house's name is a comparison between the tiny sliver of leftover land he used and the final drops of wine in a wine a bottle. He says, "There's a saying in Japanese, that the last drop of wine is considered to be lucky. That's the inspiration."[11] While Lucky Drops is an extreme example, dealing with limited space is an important part of home life for most Japanese young people. Other unique elements of Japanese life include a strong focus on being considerate of others, a love of bathing rituals, and a dedication to putting in long hours at school and at work. Japanese families are also strongly impacted by gender inequality and lingering stereotypes about the proper roles of men and women.

Living in a Small Space

Lucky Drops is unusual, but tiny houses like this are not uncommon in Japanese cities. Because the majority of Japan is mountainous and not suitable for building on, its population of more than 126 million people is concentrated in relatively small, flat areas of land. To accommodate the country's population, houses are typically small, and people learn to make the most of the available space. The website Shrink That Footprint compares average home sizes around the world. It reports that the average new home size in Japan is relatively small, at approximately 1,023 square feet (95 sq. m), which is about half the size of the typical US house.

The Japanese have adapted to living in small spaces in a number of different ways. Many apartments in the cities have bedrooms so small that a bed takes up most of the available space. As a result, people sometimes sleep on beds that can be put away during the daytime, leaving them more space for other activities. These beds are called futons. Futons are thin mattresses that are placed on the floor for sleeping at night, then folded up and stored away in a cupboard during the day. People who sleep on futons often insist that these beds are much better for their back and joints because they are much firmer than Western-style beds. Another advantage of futons is that they are much easier to keep clean. Canadian John Spacey has lived in Japan for more than ten years. He explains that Japanese people regularly shake out their futons and hang them from windows and balconies. Sometimes they even use a special bamboo stick to beat the dust out. He says, "As a result of futon culture, buildings in Japan never have a regulation against hanging clothes and beds from windows. . . . Japan's urban landscape is a sea of futons on sunny days."[12] While an increasing number of young people are opting for Western-style beds, the futon remains common in Japan.

> "As a result of futon culture, buildings in Japan never have a regulation against hanging clothes and beds from windows. . . . Japan's urban landscape is a sea of futons on sunny days."[12]
>
> —John Spacey, who has lived in Japan for more than ten years

Futons are not the only way to maximize limited space. Japanese homes are designed with other features to make living in a small space easier. For instance, many have sliding doors because they take up less space than doors that swing open. In addition, appliances such as refrigerators and stoves are often relatively small. Everyday routines are also impacted by space consciousness. For example, with less storage space for food, people usually only buy a small amount of groceries at one time. Japanese people also generally do their laundry more often, sometimes every day.

A family shares a meal at a table in a cramped kitchen. Houses are generally small in Japanese cities, and families have adapted to living in small spaces. The typical home in Japan is about half the size of the average house in the United States.

Lack of Privacy

A lack of space not only impacts the way Japanese homes are constructed and furnished, it also means that people must always be conscious of how their actions affect others. In crowded urban areas, where large numbers of people share relatively small spaces, young people learn to always be mindful of those around them, because this makes it easier to share that space. Eri Sato explains that a lack of space is a defining characteristic of everyday life in Japan. “Space has a huge impact on Japanese lifestyle.” For example, she says, “I am conscious of keeping my voice low, of generally keeping a low profile, even in my own house.”[13] She says that her family and neighbors all live in such close proximity that she definitely feels a lack of privacy.

For those people who do live on farms and in the villages of Japan’s countryside, life is markedly different. Homes are bigger, and people have more space and privacy. However, research reveals that living in the countryside is becoming less and less common in Japan, and this trend is likely to continue. In recent years, the overall population of Japan has been declining, and it is the countryside that is seeing the greatest impact of this decline. Many researchers report that Japanese villages are emptying at an alarming rate. Young people in particular are deserting these villages for the cities, where they hope for better jobs and educational opportunities. Dairy farmer Yoshihiro Shibata lives in the small village of Hara-Izumi. He talks about just how much the village has shrunk. For example, he says, "When I was young, we had about 100 kids here, but now there are just five."[14] In many small country towns, there are so few young people that they have to travel to other towns to go to school.

> "I am conscious of keeping my voice low, of generally keeping a low profile, even in my own house."[13]
>
> —Eri Sato, who lives in Japan

Bathing

Regardless of whether they live in the city or the country, Japanese people place a lot of importance on bathing. In addition to simply getting one's body clean, bath time is a way to relax and relieve stress. A Japanese bath begins with getting clean, but this does not happen inside the bathtub. Instead, a person lathers up with soap outside the bathtub, using a shower or bucket of water to rinse. Once the person is completely clean, he or she gets into a hot bath to soak. Often, more than one person uses the same bathwater. An article in *Sukiya Living Magazine* explains just how important bathing is: "The Japanese bath experience amounts to much more than simply washing off. Many Japanese people view sitting in their ofuro soaking tubs as a must-do daily ritual similar to eating or sleeping. For those individuals bathing is something that they *must* do to feel healthy and happy."[15]

People bathe in their homes, but Japan also has many public baths and hot springs where people bathe with friends, family, and even strangers. Men and women bathe separately, however. *Sukiya Living Magazine* explains the popularity of these public baths, stating, "[Many] Japanese people look at bathing as a social activity. Many parents bathe with their children, enjoying the experience and feeling it builds better relationships between family members. Even co-workers might bathe together when they go to an onsen resort on a company junket, or when they visit a hotel's *sento* public bath during a business trip."[16]

Gender Roles

The typical Japanese family consists of a mother, a father, and one child. Extended family is important to the Japanese, and in the past it was common for grandparents to live with the family. However, this is no longer the case, except in rural areas. The reason for this change is that houses and apartments in most urban areas are small and expensive, and this means that most families no longer have space for grandparents to live with them. Despite this, they continue to value their extended family, and it is common for extended family to live close by and for family members to visit often.

While there have been changes in recent years, home life in Japan is still strongly affected by traditional beliefs about the roles of men and women. Traditionally, the man in a Japanese household is the breadwinner. The woman is expected to become a mother and to raise the couple's child or children, look after the house, and manage the family's finances. Children's primary focus is on succeeding in school, and they are expected to spend long hours with classes and study. Same-sex marriage is not recognized by law in Japan. In 2015 a district in Tokyo became the first in the country to recognize same-sex partnerships; however, in most of the country same-sex couples have no legal rights and often face discrimination.

Overall, males often receive preferential treatment in Japanese culture. The World Economic Forum published a report in 2014 that measured and compared gender equality in health, education, the economy, and politics. Japan ranked comparatively low for gender equality—104 out of 142 countries analyzed (with 142 being the worst). In particular, researchers found inequality in the areas of political empowerment and workplace treatment. They report that there are very few Japanese women in parliament and that in the workplace, women earn significantly less overall and are unlikely to hold managerial positions. Becky Osawa moved from Canada to Japan to teach English, and she says that gender inequality starts young. For instance, it was very obvious at the school where she taught. She says:

> Boys were constantly deemed more important than girls. School staff never said outright that boys were more important, but actions speak louder than words. For example, in my public school's class/student lists, the boys are ALWAYS first. . . . It's not just class lists. Whenever the kids go anywhere or present themselves, whether it's just to the gym for an assembly, a school trip, Sports' Day, or graduation, the boys are always first.[17]

Osawa talks about one instance when students were casting ballots for student elections. She says that a group of girls were ready and walking to the booths to vote, but they were stopped by a teacher and told that they had to wait and let the boys go first, even though the boys were not even ready.

No Shoes in the House

In Japan it is customary to remove one's shoes before going inside. Japanese people remove their shoes at the doors to houses, schools, temples, shrines, and some other buildings, and exchange them for a pair of inside slippers. In addition, special slippers are used in the toilet room only. Removing one's shoes reduces the amount of dirt and dust that comes into the house from outside. Posting online, Mike Rogers explains this custom, stating, "My mom was Japanese. I was raised with the idea that it is unquestionably taboo to wear shoes in the house." He explains, "When you are walking around in your shoes outside, you are stepping in all sorts of dirt and debris. And when you stop to think about it, you are also stepping in all sorts of specks of animal excrement, human spittle, gum—Lord knows what else." Keeping the floor clean is particularly important in Japan because people often sit on the floor when they eat, and many sleep on futons on the floor.

Mike Rogers, "The Japanese Have No Holes in Their Socks," comment on AnthroScape Human Biodiversity Forum, "Why the Japanese Don't Wear Shoes in the House," February 26, 2013. http://s1.zetaboards.com/anthroscape.

The Role of Fathers

While Japanese men usually earn more at work, their jobs demand a lot of their time. Men typically face strong pressure to work very long hours, and it is common for a Japanese father to spend most of the weekday at work, only spending time with his children on the weekends. Writer Grace Buchele Mineta lived in Tokyo for almost three years before she and her husband moved to the countryside nearby. She says, "My husband was working 14 hour work days—and he was still one of the first people to leave the office every single day." She observes that leaving work late was extremely common. She says that sometimes when she rode the train out of the main part of Tokyo at 11:30 p.m., "the car would be packed (literally packed) with salarymen [office workers], in their black suits and falling asleep as they stood."[18] In recent years some Japanese fathers have chosen to spend more time at home; however, these men are still in the minority.

> "There's a very strong belief that a woman's place is in the home. That mothers should have sole responsibility for child raising."[20]
>
> —Linda Lim, a professor at the University of Michigan's Ross School of Business

Kaori Shoji writes for the *Japan Times*. She says that as a child, she was so used to never seeing her father that she was very surprised the first time she met a father who was not at work all the time. She says:

> I still have vivid memories of my first encounter with a non-Japanese dad. This was in the first grade, in the living room of my American friend, Mary Ellen. I was shocked to find an adult male on the premises in broad daylight, relaxing on the couch and laughing with Mary's mom. This dad . . . always sat down to meals with the family, gave birthday presents and hugs and read bedtime stories. I couldn't wrap my mind around that one.[19]

Mothers

While a father typically spends most of his time at work, the traditional role of a mother is to stay home to manage the household and care for the children. Linda Lim is a professor of strategy, business, and economic development in Asia at the University of Michigan's Ross School of Business. She explains, "There's a very strong belief that a woman's place is in the home. That mothers should have sole responsibility for child raising."[20] If current trends continue, the majority of Japanese girls can expect to give up their jobs and become stay-at-home mothers if they decide to have children. While estimates vary, researchers say that the majority of working mothers do so; a 2013 BBC News report stated that 70 percent quit when they have their first child.

Despite strong pressure to stay at home, in recent years an increasing number of women have made the decision to be working mothers. However, this decision is not usually easy. One of the biggest challenges that working mothers face is a lack of day care facilities. In a 2015 publication, Japan's Ministry of Health, Labour and Welfare reported, "At present . . . there are over 20,000 wait-listed children who wish to enter day care centers, but are unable to. The issue of wait-listed children is quite significant to parents

The traditional role of a Japanese mother is to manage the household and care for the children. The majority of working women leave their job when they have their first child.

> "At present . . . there are over 20,000 wait-listed children who wish to enter day care centers, but are unable to. The issue of wait-listed children is quite significant to parents who wish to raise their children while working."[21]
>
> —The Ministry of Health, Labour and Welfare, an office of the Japanese government

who wish to raise their children while working."[21] As a result of such long wait lists, the ministry reports that some women are forced to make a choice between work and family.

Another challenge facing working mothers is that when they take a job, like men they often are expected to put in long hours. As a result, it can be difficult to manage both a job and take care of a household and children. Kumi Matsumoto works for Japan's Ministry of Foreign Affairs. She says that because they are expected to work such long hours, working mothers often need a lot of help. "Mothers, babysitters, nursery schools," she says, "and somehow manage to do it. But I know many women couldn't do that much and just quit."[22] Yu Korekawa is a senior researcher with the Population Dynamics Research Department at Japan's National Institute of Population and Social Security Research. He agrees that work expectations make it extremely difficult to work and be a parent. "I have two babies. Two daughters—one is seven years old and the other one is just eight months," he says. "My wife is working and it's kind of very difficult."[23]

Independence and Consideration for Others

While Japanese mothers devote a lot of time to looking after their children, they also encourage them to be independent and relatively self-sufficient from a young age. For example, young children frequently ride the subway and run errands alone. Christine Gross-Loh, author of *Parenting Without Borders: Surprising Lessons Parents Around the World Can Teach Us*, talks about seeing this independence when she lived in Japan. She gives the example of ten-year-old Tomo, who lived in her neighborhood:

> Tomo . . . was incredibly independent. He had walked to school on his own since he was 6 years old, just like all Japanese 6-year-olds do. He always took meticulous

care of his belongings when he came to visit us, arranging his shoes just so when he took them off, and he taught my son how to ride the city bus. . . . When he'd come over for dinner, he offered to run out to fetch ingredients I needed, helped make the salad and stir-fried noodles.[24]

A young girl rides the subway to school by herself, which is a common occurrence in Japan, where independence and self-sufficiency are encouraged from an early age.

In addition to independence, Japanese youth quickly learn the importance of always showing consideration for others. Becky Osawa states, "Japanese people are taught from the very beginning to be considerate of others, and it's enforced to the fullest extent from preschool onward." For example, she says, "This includes always waiting in line and being quiet so that you don't disturb others. Public transit announcements always tell you to put your phone on manner mode, and talking on your phone on public transit is a major no-no."[25] In fact, she says people are often so quiet in public spaces that it is not uncommon for a crowd of people on a train to be completely silent.

Another way young people are taught to show respect for others is by respecting others' time and always being extremely punctual. For instance, youth are expected to be on time or early to classes and after-school clubs. This attention to punc-

Living in the Country

Many people report that compared to the city, life in the countryside is like taking a step back in time. Jeffrey Hays, a teacher and writer currently living in Japan, gives some examples. He says:

> Families of shop keepers often live above their shops, calculations are sometimes still made on an abacus and the wife often runs upstairs when business is slow to take care of household chores. Post offices serve as banks and insurance companies. Volunteer postmen serve as firefighters, report on potholes and traffic accidents and help out elderly people by picking up their bank books and bringing them back cash. Business in some places is conducted on a barter system known as dan-dan ("thanks again").

While some people enjoy the slower-paced lifestyle of the country, statistics show that young people are leaving it for the more modern lifestyle that Japan's cities offer.

Jeffrey Hays, "Urban and Rural Life in Japan," Facts and Details, January 2013. http://factsanddetails.com.

tuality continues throughout their lives. People who do not live in Japan are often surprised at just how important punctuality is there. An article in the *Hiragana Times* offers some observations on Japanese punctuality from visitors to that country. "Mail and parcels came punctually during the specified hours and that surprised me at first," says one person. Another comments, "Japanese people arrive at least 15 minutes before the agreed time. If you are only a little bit late, they look cross." And another says, "I was one-minute late for my part-time job, and everyone gave me the cold shoulder throughout the day."[26]

Home and family life are an important part of Japanese culture. Most families have strong ties between both immediate and extended family members, and Japanese young people are taught to always respect and care for their family members.

CHAPTER THREE

Education and Work

US high school student Candela Guo spent time in Japan as an exchange student. She found that school was a very serious affair that took up most of her time and energy every day. She explains:

> It is very different from what I was familiar with in the U.S. Here, getting up by 6am, taking the public transportation for 2 hours to commute to school (yes VERY FAR but not uncommon for kids here, I run into students in uniform at the platform 6:30am every morning), attending school for 6 periods, participating in the after school club activities for 3 hours or so, spending another 2 hours on the way home, finally going to sleep at 11 or 12pm if lucky.[27]

Other students—both exchange students and native ones—echo Guo's observations. Later, after they graduate from school and begin working, young people generally report that the long hours and hard work continue. Overall, the Japanese have a reputation for working hard at both school and work.

School

School is a central focus of life for Japanese young people. They start when they are six years old and attend elementary school for six years, middle school for three, and high school for three. Children are required to go to elementary and middle school but not high school. After high school, students can go to a two-year junior college or a four-year university. The Japan Center for Economic Research reports that more than half of high school graduates go on to college. Those students who do not, can attend a vocational school or get a job right away. However, obtaining a university degree generally guarantees a better job.

Japan has a highly educated population overall. Most young people attend school all the way through high school, and a large percentage go on to receive a college education. In a 2016 report, the Organisation for Economic Co-Operation and Development (OECD) estimated that most of Japan's young people are well educated. The OECD reported that about 80 percent of them undertake further education after high school, and the majority receive a degree. This is a high percentage compared to other countries. In contrast, however, the OECD reported that the number who receive an advanced degree such as a master's or doctorate is relatively low compared to other developed countries.

Students spend a lot of time in school. The Japanese school year starts in the beginning of April and ends in late March. Class is held on more than two hundred days a year on average, which is more than the worldwide average. Until 2002, students even attended school on Saturday, with a total of six school days a week. That year, the school week was changed to five days so that young people could have more free time. However, many students report that despite the fact that schools are no longer required to have classes on Saturday, in reality many students do continue to study or attend classes on Saturday.

Group Cohesion

The Japanese educational system strongly encourages cohesion and uniformity among students. They are expected to dress and act like their peers, and expressions of creativity or individuality are strongly discouraged. For example, students wear identical uniforms and are not usually allowed to wear makeup, jewelry, or other accessories. They are even discouraged from hairstyles that differ from their peers. Karen Ma lived in Japan for fifteen years. She says that the pressure to conform to the group is so strong that students who stand out in any way are likely to be bullied or disciplined. She explains, "Individuality is very much frowned upon. Students in Japan learn to hide their unique features to avoid being shunned." For instance, she says, "a kid with naturally lighter hair may have to dye it black. . . . Likewise, if you're super smart you would do well to hide that as well. Any attempts to answer your teacher's questions too eagerly will make your peers feel you're showing off, or trying to stand out, which is not appreciated."[28]

> "Individuality is very much frowned upon. Students in Japan learn to hide their unique features to avoid being shunned."[28]
>
> —Karen Ma, who lived in Japan for fifteen years

Grace Zhang says that she immigrated to Japan with her family and felt like her teachers and peers were constantly pressuring her to suppress her individuality and to act the same as all the other students. She says, "It felt like the school really focused on making sure that I learn the Japanese way properly. . . . They REALLY put in the effort to make sure you're just like the other Japanese children."[29] As a result, she says that she had to suppress a lot of her natural mannerisms while she was living in Japan and learn to stand, sit, eat, and even laugh just like everybody else.

Students who are unable to conform are frequently subject to bullying. Young people report that it is extremely common to be bullied, both verbally and physically, for being different in any way. For example, Japanese teenager Nanae Munemasa says that she became the target of bullying after she transferred schools for a short time. She explains that when she returned to her original school, the other students branded her as a truant and started to bully her. According to Munemasa, she was slapped in the girls' bathroom, beaten with broomsticks, and attacked while at a swimming lesson. "I was the last one to get out of the pool," she says of the swimming lesson. "A brush flew out of nowhere and it hit me underwater. I nearly drowned. I had a huge bump on my forehead."[30]

School Routines

With the exception of those who are ostracized for being different, most students become very close to their class group at school. Michael Richey spent two years living in Japan as part of a teaching exchange program. He explains, "Students generally spend all years at a given school with the same group of

Youths in Japan spend a lot of time in school—more than two hundred days a year on average. The Japanese educational system encourages cohesion and uniformity among students.

classmates. This [group] resides in one room, cleans that room, eats in that room, and sometimes even decorates it. . . . The end result is that school groups become a family in and of themselves."[31] Since students usually stay in one room for the entire school day, various teachers usually come to them in order to teach each school subject.

At lunchtime most elementary and middle school students eat the same meal together in their classroom, which is prepared by the school cafeteria. A typical school lunch includes rice, vegetables, fish or chicken, and soup. Even teachers frequently eat the same meal as their students. It is usually not until high school that students bring a box lunch from home. At lunchtime the students take turns to help serve the meal to the class. *Washington Post* writer Chico Harlan describes the lunch scene at one Japanese school:

> Lunchtime, on this particular day, begins with a call from the teacher. "People in charge, please come up." Six third-graders put on their white sanitary smocks and caps and take their positions behind serving trays. One child eyes the thick reservoir of Sichuan tofu and wiggles his right arm, as if to warm up his ladling hand. A teacher shows the girl serving rice how much to give each of her classmates.[32]

Schools have no vending machines or other places to get food, so children must eat the same meal as everybody else or go hungry.

In addition to helping serve food at lunchtime, students also help keep their schools clean. During most school days a specific time is devoted to cleaning, and at that time both students and teachers work together to dust, scrub, and sweep. Michael Auslin, resident scholar and director of Japanese studies at the American Enterprise Institute, explains that cleaning time is not just about keeping the school clean. He says that it is actually a part of the students' education. "School is not just for learning from a book," he insists, "It's about learning how to become a member of society and taking responsibility for oneself."[33] By cleaning their school, students learn how to clean up after themselves and how to work together. Junior high student Kylie Igarashi says that cleaning has made her be more considerate of others. She explains, "I've . . . learned to keep my surroundings a little more clean. Even when it's not my turn to clean, it makes me feel bad to know that my friend will be the one erasing all the doodles off of my desk. It's a constant, joint effort by all of us."[34] In addition, she says that while

> "Students generally spend all years at a given school with the same group of classmates. This [group] resides in one room, cleans that room, eats in that room, and sometimes even decorates it."[31]
>
> —Michael Richey, who lived in Japan as part of a teaching exchange program

Corporal Punishment

Although corporal punishment is against the law in Japan, it does occur sometimes. In 2013 the *Japan Times* reported that an average of sixty-eight students are physically punished by their teachers each day. In recent years, there have been a number of well-publicized incidents where corporal punishment actually resulted in severe harm to students. Yoshio Sugimoto is a university professor and author of *An Introduction to Japanese Society*. She gives some examples:

> In 2013, in a high school in Osaka, as a training method a male teacher coaching basketball repeatedly hit and kicked the captain of the school team, who killed himself in despair. In 2009, in a high school in the same city, a male teacher in *kendo* (Japanese fencing), infuriated by a female student's behavior, punched her in the face and clubbed her with a bamboo sword several times, resulting in her suffering a sprained neck and a ruptured eardrum. A male high school teacher in Gunma Prefecture who coached a female volleyball team inflicted similar violence on a student who later suffered from such severe depression that she could not attend school.

Yoshio Sugimoto, *An Introduction to Japanese Society.* Port Melbourne, Australia: Cambridge University Press, 2014, p. 147.

cleaning might not sound fun, it is actually a positive experience most of the time. "Cleaning time is not only hard-core scrubbing and polishing, but mostly students chatting about today's events, throwing toilet paper at each other (even though we have to clean that as well, which is why we stop doing that as we grow older), and the teacher poking fun at how slow we are."[35] She says that her teacher always encourages the students while they clean and often makes jokes in order to make the job feel easier.

Exams

While cleaning and food prep are typical parts of the school day for most Japanese students, their primary focus is exams, which are critical to their education and future careers. The best way to get a good job in Japan is to get into a good university, and in order to get into a good university, a student must do well on the university entrance exams. Yoshio Sugimoto, professor emerita in

Students make their way to the University of Tokyo where they will take the university entrance exams. Japanese students spend much of their time preparing for exams, which are critical to their education and future careers.

the School of Social Sciences and Communications at La Trobe University in Melbourne, Australia, explains that when companies are looking for new employees, they place a lot of importance on which university the students attended. She says that many large and prestigious firms will not even consider students who graduated from mediocre universities. Sugimoto says:

> Approximately half of all major companies target only a small number of top universities for the recruitment of fresh employees. Corporations justify the system on the grounds that, in the absence of dependable detailed information about the quality of each student, the most reliable

> indicator is the level of the university which he or she has succeeded in entering: the more difficult it is to get in, the more ability the prospective employee must have.[36]

This means that it is extremely important for students to do well on their exams so that they can attend a good university.

However, university entrance exams are not the only important exams that Japanese students must take. High schools also admit students based on exam results. Michael Richey explains that because schools are so competitive, the focus on exams can start even before junior high school. He explains, "To get a good job in Japan, you need to go to a good university. To get into a good university, you need to pass that university's entrance exams. The universities you can apply for depend on the high school you attended. To get into a good high school, you need [to] pass the high school entrance exams. And prep for those usually start in junior high, but can start much earlier."[37] Because tests are so important, students often end up spending much of their school years focused on preparing for exams.

> "Approximately half of all major companies target only a small number of top universities for the recruitment of fresh employees."[36]
>
> —Yoshio Sugimoto, professor emerita at La Trobe University in Melbourne, Australia

Cram Schools and Universities

In order to increase their chances of doing well on their exams, many students attend private cram schools, called *juku*, after their regular school hours. Some cram schools teach nonacademic subjects like sports or arts, but the majority are focused on helping students do well on exams. Writer for the *Japan Times* Louise George Kittaka describes the experience of Manami, a sixth grader who lives in Tokyo: "For the past year . . . Manami has had dinner at home an average of four times a week. The rest of the time she has had to make do with a juku-ben, a boxed dinner prepared by her mother and consumed between classes at juku, or cram school." Kittaka says that Manami has been attending cram school since third grade, with the goal of getting into a private junior high school. In addition to going three weekday evenings, she spends most of Saturday there. Kittaka says, "Three years of late nights, limited free time and piles of homework culminated in a round of entrance exams last month. Manami passed the test to attend her school of choice and can now finally relax and enjoy the remaining few weeks of elementary school with her friends."[38] While some students like Manami start attending cram school in the elementary grades, most wait until high school, when it comes time to prepare for university entrance exams.

While students in elementary through high school face extreme pressure to study hard and do well on their exams, when they get to college many have the opportunity for a break. This is because many companies pick employees based on the ranking of the university they attend, not what they study or the grades they get. As a result, many students find that they do not need to study hard, because it makes little difference to their job prospects. College students report that it is common to sleep or talk during lectures and that many students skip lectures entirely. Teachers frequently allow this behavior by not expecting much from their students. Keisuke Fujita is an education and human sciences major at Yokohama National University. He says that he spends very little time studying, stating, "I don't study for classes, except when I have assignments due."[39] In 2012 education company Benesse Corporation conducted a survey that showed that Fujita's experience is typical. It reports that two-thirds of Japanese university students study for two hours or less outside of class each week.

Finding a Job After School

Whether or not they obtain a college degree, an increasing number of young people in Japan are experiencing problems when it comes time to find a job. A growing percentage are unable to obtain full-time jobs and must settle for temporary or part-time positions that pay much less. The biggest reason for this is that due to economic concerns, many Japanese companies have stopped hiring regular employees in recent years and hire part-time workers instead because they are cheaper and easier to fire. Making the situation even worse is the fact that

Respect for Elders

In Japanese culture, it is extremely important for people to show respect to their elders, and school is no exception. In addition to respecting teachers, students are expected to show respect to older students, even if those students are only a year ahead of them. US high school exchange student Candela Guo explains, "The first year [students] are obligated to bow and greet . . . students who are in second and third years, and the new members are always responsible for cleaning the room and carrying heavy equipment." Japanese blogger Yuta Aoki talks about being in the youngest grade when entering junior high and and describes how strange it was at first to treat the older students as superiors. Aoki says, "Suddenly, we were obligated to use polite speech with 8th and 9th graders. We needed to act like they were superiors even if we used to be friends and play together."

Candela Guo, "The Busy Life of a Student Studying in Japan," Greenheart Travel, 2013. https://greenhearttravel.org.

Yuta Aoki, "What Is It like Growing Up in Japan?," *Quora*, December 3, 2014. www.quora.com.

because the culture places so much importance on respecting one's elders, older workers hold a large percentage of the permanent jobs. This means that many young job seekers are left with part-time jobs. According to a labor ministry survey, people with part-time jobs now account for 40 percent of the nation's workforce. "Job prospects for young people throughout Japan today are really awful,"[40] says Kyle Cleveland, associate director of Temple University–Japan's Institute of Contemporary Asian Studies.

Another problem facing many young job seekers is that they are realizing they do not like Japan's existing job culture, but they can find few good alternatives. The majority of Japanese companies expect employees to work extremely long hours, and an increasing number of young people are rebelling against that. Unfortunately, there is a scarcity of better options. For example, a young woman named Kyoko says that while she was in college, she interviewed with ten different companies but realized that she simply did not want to work extremely

A growing number of young people are unable to obtain full-time jobs and must settle for part-time positions that pay much less. As a result nearly half of Japan's young people have moved back in with their parents.

long hours in the corporate world like her father had. "I realized that wasn't who I wanted to be," says Kyoko. However, she laments, "Why has being myself cost me so dearly?"[41] By making the choice not to enter the corporate world, she said that she has been forced to hold a string of lower-paying part-time jobs because this is all she can find.

Financial Hardship

Many of Japan's teens and young adults struggle to find good jobs and earn decent wages after they leave school. Shigeyuki Jo, coauthor of "The Truth of Generational Inequalities," says, "There is a feeling among young generations that no matter how hard we try, we can't get ahead." Jo insists, "Every avenue seems to be blocked, like we're butting our heads against a wall."[42]

Because Japanese society places so much importance on belonging to a group, the lack of a permanent job can be a particular hardship. David Slater, associate professor of Japanese studies at Tokyo's Sophia University, explains, "Who you are and what you are in Japan is a function of where you work and the obligations that you have to your workmates. . . . If you lose that, you lose a lot more than just your wage. You lose your identity within society. . . . If you are drifting from one job to another, people look at you like you are morally suspect—and you look at yourself the same way."[43]

Many young adults are finding that their jobs pay so little that they have to move back in with their parents. According to a 2016 Pew Research Center report, the number of twenty- to thirty-four-year-olds living with their parents in Japan increased from about 30 percent in 1980 to almost 50 percent in 2012. One thirty-two-year-old freelance writer has been living with his parents since he was twenty-five because he cannot afford to live alone. He considers himself to be fairly lucky, because "unlike many others in my situation, I have a pretty good relationship with my parents."[44] Another young man who was interviewed by a reporter says he does not feel so lucky. He says that living with his parents is very difficult because they want to know about everything he does. For instance, he says, "If I were to tell them I don't need a dinner one certain night, I'd need to explain why. If I came back home late, they would ask me what I was doing." He complains, "It feels like I'm under their constant surveillance."[45]

> "If you are drifting from one job to another, people look at you like you are morally suspect—and you look at yourself the same way."[43]
>
> —David Slater, associate professor at Tokyo's Sophia University

Despite problems such as this, many people speak positively about Japan's schools and workplaces. Overall, its population is hardworking and well educated. Experts agree that 99 percent of the population is literate. And despite complaints about the job market, Japanese young people face a relatively low unemployment rate compared to many other countries. The country even attracts a large number of foreigners who want to attend school or work there.

CHAPTER FOUR

Social Life

When asked about their social lives, Japanese young people report interests similar to young people all over the world: They listen to music, hang out with friends, play sports, and go shopping. However, many of their activities have a decidedly Japanese spin to them. For example, one of the most popular girl bands in Japan is BABYMETAL. This musical group has a style unlike any other. It has combined heavy metal, death metal, and pop music to create an unusual blend of dark and cute. Journalist Micah Nathan describes a performance: "A trio of chipper, hyper-choreographed Japanese girls harmonizing and talk-singing about eating chocolate. . . . The guitars shredded, the drums did that blast beat thing, the girls—lead singer Su-metal, backup singers Yuimetal and Moametal—screamed and danced and looked both super-cute and super-serious."[46] BABYMETAL is one of a multitude of Japanese groups that are part of a style known as Japanese pop, or J-pop. J-pop fuses Western influences such as pop and rock with the traditional music of Japan. It is just one example of the way culture influences the social lives of young people in Japan.

School Influences

While Japanese young people enjoy many of the same activities as youth in other Westernized countries, their social lives are not entirely their own. Commenting online, Miyuki E. says, "For the most part, while you are a teenager in Japan, school is your life." Many schools require students to participate in after-school clubs, or *bukatsu*. These clubs appeal to many different interests. At her school, Miyuki E. explains, "we have many social clubs that range from sports like soccer, kendo, even [badminton] , to singing clubs, reading clubs, anime clubs, video game clubs . . . etc." As a result of these clubs, students typically have little free time after school.

She says, "School ends at 3 or 4, but then you stay for your club until sometime [around] 6 or 7 at night. My friend was in the Shuji club, (Japanese calligraphy) and sometimes she left at 8 pm!"[47]

Joanne G. Yoshida, the mother of another Japanese student, also talks about the fact that after-school clubs take up so much time that young people often have little time to do anything else. She says:

> My daughter, for example, joined basketball club. After school finishes at 4pm she changes directly into her gym clothes, *tai-so fuku* . . . and heads to the *tai-iku-kan* . . . school gymnasium. She finishes club at 6.30pm and by the time she cleans up and gets home it is 7pm. On the weekends, there is *bukatsu* on both days, and on summer vacation *bukatsu* continues for morning or afternoon practice, with the exception of a few days off on the O-bon holiday and occasional single days off.[48]

The mother of another Japanese student comments that her son has so much homework that "he does more hours [of work] than I do."[49]

The popular Japanese girl band BABYMETAL plays a show in Berkshire, Britain. The group is part of a musical style known as J-pop, which fuses Western pop and rock with traditional Japanese music.

However, while after-school clubs do take up a lot of time, Japanese young people typically report that they enjoy their chosen club and that it becomes a central part of their social life. Even college students have the opportunity to participate in bukatsu. University student Marie Hayashi Strand is on the ski team at her school and says that she enjoys the strong social bonds that she has developed with her team members. "I love my ski team, and when I state that I am a member, I do so with pride,"[50] she says.

Smartphones and Social Media

In between (and sometimes in the middle of) their many planned activities, Japanese young people spend time messaging, visiting social media, and playing games on their phones. Smartphones are everywhere in Japan. In a 2015 survey, information security firm Digital Arts found that approximately 96 percent of Japanese high school students and 60 percent of junior high students have a mobile phone. Researchers found that girls spend about seven hours a day on their phones, and boys spend about four. Eighteen-year-old Sumire says she rarely, if ever, disconnects from her phone. "I'm online from the moment I wake up until I go to sleep, whenever I have time—even in class," she says. "I'm always messaging friends on LINE, even when I'm in the bath. I guess I feel lonely if I'm not online, sort of disconnected."[51]

"I'm always messaging friends on LINE, even when I'm in the bath. I guess I feel lonely if I'm not online, sort of disconnected."[51]

—Sumire, a Japanese teenager

Social media is so popular that many Japanese young people aspire to be a social media star. A recent survey of fourth-grade boys in Osaka, for instance, asked what they want to be when they grow up. The most popular choices were soccer player, doctor, and YouTuber (in that order).

Among the many social media options, one stands out as most popular among Japanese youth. That site, called LINE, is a mobile message app that allows users to make voice and video calls, send messages, and share pictures, music, and videos. Osaka-based journalist Brian Ashcraft says, "In Japan, young people often swap LINE IDs like only a few years ago

Being Part of a Group

While fitting in socially is important to young people all over the world, belonging to a social group is particularly important to many Japanese young people because of the emphasis that Japanese culture places on groups. As they grow up, youth are taught to think of themselves as part of various groups—for instance, class groups at school, a sports team, or after-school clubs—and are strongly encouraged to act in a way that helps them blend in with that group. As a result, expressions of individuality are often discouraged, because they disrupt group conformity. The common Japanese saying "The nail that sticks up gets hammered down" means that anyone who stands out will be pressured to conform. Japanese teenager Nanae Munemasa explains that this pressure is very strong and that people are often treated unkindly until they do conform. She says, "In Japan, you have to fall in line with other people. And if you cannot do that, you're either ignored or bullied."

Quoted in Rebecca Wright, "Japan's Worst Day for Teen Suicides," CNN, September 1, 2015. www.cnn.com.

they'd swap email addresses or phone numbers."[52] LINE has many features that appeal to young people. For example, users can easily create short videos accompanied by background music to share with their friends. Another feature teens like is the "shake it" function, where friends can add one another to their contact lists simply by standing close together and shaking their phones. One of the most popular features of LINE, though, is that it lets users send virtual stickers to their friends. These stickers are like giant emoji. Japanese youth use stickers to show their feelings, express their own distinct personality, or sometimes just to show the stickers off. Stickers are usually sold in sets of twelve to eighteen, at a dollar or two per set, and feature thousands of different characters ranging from cute to bizarre. New stickers are continually released, and they are extremely popular among young people.

Another reason that LINE is so popular among Japanese young people is that it is chat based, so it offers more privacy than many other social networking sites. Private or anonymous types of social media are most popular among young people in

Japan. This is because Japanese culture places a lot of importance on privacy and modesty, and Japanese young people are generally cautious about publicly posting anything on social media when they know that strangers will see it. In addition to LINE, Twitter is another popular site among Japanese youth because it allows anonymity. Ryan Broderick is a reporter for BuzzFeed News. He explains, "Japanese Twitter users prefer anonymity; it is rare to see someone use their real name as their username and it's even rarer to find someone who is using their own face as their avatar."[53] Unlike Twitter, Facebook does not allow anonymity, and it is not very popular among young people in Japan.

Teenage Cultural Trends

In addition to spending hours a day using social media, most Japanese youth—particularly girls—love all things cute. Cute culture is known as *kawaii*, and it is everywhere in Japan. Japanese girls wear cute clothes and fashion accessories, decorate their bedrooms with cute items, and strive for cuteness in their hairstyles. Many teenage girls would prefer to be called cute rather than pretty or sexy. Manami Okazaki and Geoff Johnson are the authors of *Kawaii! Japan's Culture of Cuteness*. They explain, "Kawaii things are usually soft, bright, round and small. They aren't aggressive or belligerent: they give you peace of mind and a sense of security."[54] The Hello Kitty brand is an example of cute. The huggable, white, cat-inspired character is found on thousands of products in Japan, including toys, bedding, office supplies, clothing, jewelry, and electronics. In addition to Hello Kitty, there are countless other cute characters in Japan. Okazaki and Johnson talk about the pervasiveness of cuteness, commenting that it is possible to find almost any consumer item with a cute character on it. They ask, "Where else in the world can you find cute public buses, frying pans, golf balls, fans, motorcycle helmets, cars, planes and AC adaptors with dopey-looking bears emblazoned on them?"[55]

> "Kawaii things are usually soft, bright, round and small. They aren't aggressive or belligerent: they give you peace of mind and a sense of security."[54]
>
> —Manami Okazaki and Geoff Johnson, authors of *Kawaii! Japan's Culture of Cuteness*

A young woman in the Harajuku district of Tokyo dresses in Harajuku style, a popular trend that celebrates extreme and unique fashion and costumes.

Another trend embraced by youth in Japan is Harajuku culture. Harajuku culture is centered in the Harajuku district of Tokyo. Here teens like to hang out and to show off extreme and unique fashion and costumes known as Harajuku. This style is extremely imaginative and combines multiple styles, including kawaii. For instance, one popular type of Harajuku style is the Lolita, which is based on Victorian style. Girls in Lolita style might wear ruffles and lace, bows, and knee socks. Another type of Harajuku style, cosplay, involves dressing up as a well-known character from a book, movie, or game. Boys also dress in Harajuku style. For example, a recent fashion trend among some boys is a genderless look. Harajuku style is so extreme that people who have never seen it before are often surprised. On Sundays, the Harajuku district is overflowing with youth dressed up in a multitude of different Harajuku styles. One visitor to Japan comments, "We were completely unprepared for what we found. The area around the [Harajuku] station was just

Public Affection

On a typical US high school campus at lunchtime, or anywhere else that teens gather, it is not uncommon to see young couples hugging and kissing. This would be an unlikely sight in Japan. Even when in a serious relationship, Japanese couples rarely show a lot of physical affection in public. "In general, Japanese people don't show as much affection towards each other in public (or in private, for that matter) compared to Western couples. This surprises a lot of people at first. There's a lack of hand holding, hugging, kissing, and so on in public places," writes one blog author. He put out a survey on the topic and says that a number of Japanese girls responded with explanations for this lack of affection. Their explanations included, "It's more important to understand each other than it is to show how much I love someone through touching," and, "Less physical contact makes physical contact more special when it happens. If you always touch each other, then it's not special anymore when you do." Other people argue that the lack of public expression is because many Japanese couples express their feelings in a more subtle and indirect way compared with other cultures.

Koichi, "What It's Like Dating a Japanese Girl," *Tofugu* (blog), October 16, 2013. www.tofugu.com.

packed with people shoulder to shoulder and some of the costumes were seriously over the top. The favorite of the day seemed to be the Strawberry themed 'Sweet Lolita' characters, but we also saw plenty of Gothic Lolitas and a couple sailor types."[56]

Dating

Just as Japan has developed its own unique fashion, it has some unique dating customs. Dating traditionally starts with a declaration of love called *kokuhaku*. This is when one person confesses love for another person and asks that person to go out with him or her. If the other person agrees, the two are considered to officially be a couple. Writing in the Japanese magazine *Kansai Scene*, one author explains how it works: "The most basic way of confessing this is to say, 'Sukidesu. Tsukiattekudasai.' . . . This translates to, 'I love you, can we start seeing each other?' It marks the beginning of a serious boyfriend/girlfriend relationship. You may have hung out with the person a few times, but your relationship hasn't technically started until this confession of love is made."[57] Mami Suzuki is Japanese and researches who writes for the *Tofugu* blog. She talks about the advantages of this custom, explaining that it helps make the relationship clear from the beginning. "Because of this," she says, "we don't usually need to have that awkward moment of asking 'Are we serious about each other?' or 'Are we exclusive?' or even 'Do you love me?'"[58] Instead, she says, by making and accepting declarations of love, people know what is expected of them.

A number of studies show that a large and growing number of Japanese young people actually do not date—nor do they want to. One recent survey found that almost 30 percent of men and women in their twenties had no experience dating somebody of the opposite sex. And a study by the Japan Family Planning Association revealed that 45 percent of women and 25 percent of men ages sixteen to twenty-four were not interested in sexual contact. The most common reason that these young people gave for their aversion to dating and sex is that they do not want to deal with the work and family pressures that come with marriage. Others report that they simply find it less complicated to avoid dating. A reporter for the *Guardian* talked to two young adults about this topic. Emi Kuwahata, age twenty-three, and Eri Asada, age twenty-two, live in Tokyo. Kuwahata told the reporter, "I don't have time for a regular boyfriend. I'm trying to become a fashion designer." Asada told the reporter, "I gave up dating three years ago. I don't miss boyfriends or sex. I don't even like holding hands."[59]

Hikikomori

A significant and increasing percentage of Japanese young people not only avoid dating, but they are withdrawing completely from all social contact. These youth suffer from a phenomenon known as *hikikomori*. Translated as "withdrawn," hikikomori is when young people isolate themselves in their bedrooms for a long period of time, not leaving for school, work, or even to spend time with friends. While this kind of isolation happens to young people all over the world, it is believed to be a particularly big problem in Japan. In 2016 the Japanese government released statistics on hikikomori, reporting that Japan has approximately 541,000 hikikomori aged fifteen to nineteen. Experts believe that the reason so many young people retreat from society is that Japanese culture exerts very strong pressure on them to succeed and also to conform to the group. Those who are unable to do so sometimes choose to isolate themselves from society instead.

Yuto Onish says that he became a hikikomori after the embarrassment of failing as a team leader in a school activity. He spent eight years living in his bedroom, sleeping, reading, and surfing the Internet. "I knew it was abnormal but I didn't want to change. . . . It felt safe,"[60] he says. *Wall Street Journal* reporter Shirley S. Wang describes the experience of Ms. Kimura (who chose not to share her first name). She says, "When the Kimura family moved [to Fukuoka] from Tokyo, their middle school–aged daughter missed her old friends. Midway into her first year in high school, she stopped going. Between 14 and 19, she barely left the house, and for one year hardly left her room, interacting only with her parents."[61]

Difficulty for Those Who Are Different

Hikikomori is not the only example of young people struggling because of social pressures to conform. Japan can be a difficult place for young people who find themselves different from the majority of their peers in any way. For example, gay and lesbian teens often face social disapproval. The *Guardian* newspaper asked readers to share their experiences with being lesbian, gay, bisexual, and transgender, and one respondent explains that homosexuality is often frowned upon in Japan simply because it deviates from the norm. She says, "The major opposition to homosexuality (and lesbians in particular) is not so much that it is seen as 'wrong' or 'sinful' . . . more that it is just 'different.' The overwhelming assumption of my female students (and male ones to a lesser degree) is that they will marry, have children, give up work to be a . . . housewife."[62] She says that anyone who deviates from that lifestyle is looked upon with disapproval.

> "Japanese society is of one nation, one language and one culture. There is a saying: 'The nail that sticks out gets hammered down.'"[63]
>
> —Yumi Nakata, a mixed-race resident of Japan

Participants march in the Tokyo Rainbow Pride parade in 2016. Gay and lesbian youths in Japan often face social disapproval simply because homosexuality deviates from the norm.

Young people of mixed race or ethnicity are often viewed with disapproval, too. Only a small percentage of Japan's population is mixed race or ethnicity; the rest are almost entirely ethnic Japanese. Yumi Nakata says that she is half Japanese, which she says is often referred to as *hafu* in Japan. She says that it is very difficult to be hafu, explaining, "Japanese society is of one nation, one language and one culture. There is a saying: 'The nail that sticks out gets hammered down.' And Hafu children are often bullied in school just because they are different."[63]

Many mixed-ethnicity children in Japan report that they face difficulties throughout their lives simply because they look different from their peers. For instance, Nakata talks about the process of finding a job, stating, "Many conservative Japanese firms are still reluctant to hire Hafu, especially those who obviously look mixed. It doesn't matter if they speak perfect Japanese, many companies feel that for a position that requires you to deal with Japanese customers, you must also be Japanese."[64] She believes that she was lucky that her mother was Asian and not Caucasian, because this helps her look more ethnically Japanese and makes it easier to blend in.

Overall, most Japanese young people have busy lives filled with both schoolwork and social activities. They share many of the interests of young people all over the world, such as hanging out with friends and using social media. However, Japanese youth culture is also unique in many ways. Japan is the birthplace of a number of distinctive trends, including J-pop music, Harajuku fashion, and kawaii culture. When it comes to social media, Japan's youth favor their own social media platform, LINE, over others with huge followings outside of Japan. So although Japanese young people have a lot in common with young people around the world, they also have a culture that is very much their own.

CHAPTER FIVE

Religion

Meiji Shrine is a Shinto shrine in Tokyo. It is one of the most popular shrines in Japan. According to a 2015 article in the *Japan Times*, it receives more than 10 million visitors a year. Some of these visitors are tourists, but a large number are Tokyo residents who regularly go to the shrine. In fact, almost every town in Japan has at least one shrine or temple, and some cities have hundreds or even thousands of them. Japanese young people visit these places on a regular basis for numerous reasons, including to pray to ancestors, commemorate important occasions, and ask for good luck. Visiting shrines and temples is only one way that religion is integrated into daily life in Japan. Religious practices are important to both daily affairs and special occasions, and overall, religion plays an important part in the lives of Japanese youth.

Buddhism and Shintoism

Shintoism is Japan's oldest and most popular religion. In fact, it is believed to have been around for as long as Japanese culture has. This religion has no founder or sacred books. Instead, Shintoism is primarily a set of rituals that regulate the interactions between the living and the spirits. It is based on the belief that all living things contain spirits, or *kami*. It is believed that there are millions of kami and that they have the power to influence human life and natural forces. Youth are taught that if they treat these spirits properly and follow the proper rituals, the spirits may fulfill their requests and wishes for things such as having good health or passing an exam. Kami are believed to live in shrines, and every town has at least one shrine dedicated to the local kami. Japanese people visit shrines when they want good luck or a favor from the kami. Some people also have a small shrine in their own home. One of Shinto's kami is so popular that it even inspired a video game. The action-adventure game *Okami* features the kami Amaterasu, who takes the form of a white wolf.

While Shintoism is focused on life in the present, Buddhism—Japan's other popular religion—is focused on the soul and the afterlife. Buddhism originated in India, but it was introduced to Japan in the sixth century and adopted by the Japanese. While the Japanese people practice Shinto rituals in an effort to influence their daily lives, they primarily turn to Buddhism when somebody dies. Ian Reader, an expert on Japanese culture, explains why: "There's a traditional belief in Japan that when you die, your spirit becomes—if it's properly cared for—becomes a family ancestor. And the tradition has been for families to do Buddhist rituals at death to memorialize the dead person, to turn them into an ancestor."[65] In an effort to take care of their loved ones' spirits after death, the majority of Japanese people conduct Buddhist funerals.

> "There's a traditional belief in Japan that when you die, your spirit becomes . . . a family ancestor. And the tradition has been for families to do Buddhist rituals at death to memorialize the dead person, to turn them into an ancestor."[65]
>
> —Ian Reader, an expert on Japanese culture

At a traditional Buddhist funeral, young people play a role in helping care for the spirits of deceased family members. After services to honor the deceased, family members remain to oversee the cremation of the body. The entire family, including small children, watches as the body—inside a burnable casket—is slid into the cremation chamber. They wait in another room while the process takes place, then they are called back to finish the process of caring for the deceased family member. Osaka-based journalist Alan Wiren explains what happens next: "The crematory staff will usually give a kind of guided tour of the bones, pointing out indicators of disease and the effect of medicines."[66] After that all family members are given pairs of special chopsticks, and they start the process of picking up the bones and depositing them into an urn. They begin with the feet and end with the head so that the deceased will be comfortable.

Wiren explains that picking up the bones is also believed to give good luck to the living: "Everyone, from the grey haired to toddlers, takes up chopsticks and transfers bones to a small pot. Mothers may encourage their children to take bones from the head to foster their intelligence. Others may take up certain bones to combat illness or injury."[67]

Religion in Everyday Life

Religion is an important part of life in Japan, but for most young people and adults, it offers guidance for how to live rather than what to believe. The dominant faiths in Japan are Shintoism and Buddhism. According to *The World Factbook*, about 80 percent of Japanese people say they follow Shintoism, and about 67 percent follow Buddhism. But unlike people in many other countries and cultures, the Japanese people often follow both faiths. Which ritual or practice they engage in is guided by the particular need or situation. Shinto priest Katsutoshi Tadokoro describes

Christian Weddings

While less than 1 percent of Japan's population follows Christianity, a large percentage of couples choose to have Christian-style weddings rather than traditional Shinto-style ones. The typical Shinto wedding ceremony is limited to only a small group of family and close friends and takes place at a shrine. The bride and groom wear special wedding kimonos. Most couples explain their choice as mainly a matter of style; they prefer the more modern, relaxed, and romantic feel of a Christian wedding to the more serious Shinto style. As one young Japanese woman writes, she and her fiancé opted for a Christian-style wedding precisely for this reason: "If we had thought about our parents, we would have had a Japanese style ceremony but we are young, we wanted a more casual style." Another young woman describes the reasons behind the Christian-style weddings of many of her friends. She explains, "Many Japanese girls want to have a wedding like a European film, in a beautiful chapel, walk through the aisle in the white dress with her father. This is a dream for many girls."

Quoted in AFP/Francoise Kadri, "Christian Marriages Increasingly the Norm in Japan," Things Asian, April 16, 2003. http://thingsasian.com.

Juju Kurihara, "How Japanese People Get Married?," *Iromegane* (blog), April 18, 2015. www.iromegane.com.

> "When you're born or have a baby, people do Shinto rites. . . . When you die the ceremony is Buddhist. This is religion, Japan-style."[68]
>
> —Katsutoshi Tadokoro, a Shinto priest

how many Japanese people observe both faiths, in the context of rituals for major life events. "When you're born or have a baby, people do Shinto rites," he says. "When you die the ceremony is Buddhist. This is religion, Japan-style."[68]

Although participation in religious rituals is quite common in Japan, many Japanese actually describe themselves as not religious. A 2014 survey, for instance, found that 31 percent of Japanese people interviewed claimed to be atheists, meaning that they do not believe in the existence of God or gods. Even those who say they are not adherents of any particular faith often do follow religious traditions and engage in various religious rituals. Journalist Chris Betros, who has lived in Japan for thirty years, says this is very common—among youth and adults alike. He writes:

> Most Japanese I know say they do not believe in a deity or profess to follow any religion. Yet they go in droves to shrines during O-bon and New Year [festivals]. Prayers are written on votive tablets at shrines on the eve of important exams, Coming-of-Age Day, a job interview or in the quest for a suitable husband or wife. Furthermore, Shinto priests are always on hand to bless baseball teams before spring training begins, and at ground-breaking ceremonies for new buildings, or when machinery or vehicles that have been in use for a long time, are retired.[69]

Shrines

When visitors to shrines want to make wishes or offer prayers, they typically buy *Ema,* which are wooden plaques on which they write down their wishes and prayers. The *Ema* are then left at the shrine. Michael Holtz, a writer for the *Christian Science Monitor*, talks about some of the wishes that he has seen displayed at the Meiji Shrine in Tokyo. He says they included "prayers for a swift recovery from illness, a long-awaited job promotion, and tickets to see Arashi, a popular Japanese boy band. 'I wish for all my wishes to come true,' read one."[70]

In their visits to shrines, many Japanese youth also enjoy reading their fortunes. Typically, a visitor will spend a dollar or two for a fortune. The usual way to get a fortune is to choose a stick from a box full of different sticks. The sticks are numbered, and they coordinate with numbered drawers in a box. Depending on what number he or she selects, the person takes a piece of paper from one of the drawers, and that paper has a fortune written on it. Some shrines also have vending machines that dispense fortunes. While it is possible to purchase a fortune at any time,

Ema, *wooden plaques on which people write down their prayers and wishes, are displayed at the Meiji Shrine in Tokyo, one of the most popular shrines in Japan.*

people most commonly do so at the beginning of the year or at important milestones in their life such as taking an important exam or starting a new job.

Japanese youth also love to purchase lucky charms. In fact, charms are popular among people of all ages in Japan. Called *omamori*, these charms are believed to bring good luck or protection, and they are so popular that they are even sold in vending machines in some places. There are many different types of omamori available, including charms for happiness, love, safe travel, good luck in school, and good health. Omamori are believed to work best when they are close to a person, and it is common to see them on backpacks or even to see students holding on to them before important exams. Verity Lane spent three years living in Japan. She talks about these charms, explaining that people must continually buy new ones: "Omamori have a limited lifespan. They are usually considered only effective for one year, or until they become damaged. If something bad happened to the omamori, it breaks or gets destroyed, then it's doing its job. Especially with *migawari omamori* . . . which acts as a 'scapegoat,' the thinking goes that the bad things happen to the omamori and not to you."[71] She says that these charms should be replaced every year or they will run out of power or absorb too much bad luck. In Japan it is common to see both young people and pets with charms attached to them in some way.

"Shinto priests are always on hand to bless baseball teams before spring training begins, and at ground-breaking ceremonies for new buildings, or when machinery or vehicles that have been in use for a long time, are retired."[69]

—Journalist Chris Betros, who has lived in Japan for thirty years

Festivals

Another way that religion plays a role in the lives of Japanese young people is through festivals. There are thousands of different festivals celebrated in Japan. Among the most popular festivals are those that celebrate the New Year and the arrival of the cherry blossoms, but most festivals are connected in some way to shrines or temples and the spirits that reside in these sacred places.

People crowd a main street in Tokyo during the New Year celebration, which takes place from the first to the third of January and is the most popular of Japan's festivals.

Festivals are usually big celebrations. Participants often dress up and parade through the streets, sometimes carrying the shrine's kami with them. In addition, there is often music, food, dancing, and carnival games. Blogger Ayumi describes the Summer Obon Festival, which is a celebration to honor one's ancestors. "The festival is super popular during the summer," she writes, "and many delicious street foods can be enjoyed, such as Takoyaki

Obon

Obon is one of Japan's most popular festivals. It is celebrated in July or August, depending on where one lives, and is a Buddhist festival devoted to remembering the dead and celebrating family ties. It is believed that the spirits of the ancestors come down to visit the living at this time, and people often travel to their ancestral family homes to visit family graves. Amy Chavez lives on a small island in Japan. She describes the beginning of the festival:

> On the first day of Obon, people set out lanterns, the light of which is meant to guide the spirits back to their homes. These electrified paper lanterns (or sometimes very small fires lit outside the home) are placed inside the house or, if it's the first Bon holiday after a family member has passed away, it will be more conspicuously placed outside the house to help the spirit find its way back for the first time.

In addition to lighting lanterns, families clean their ancestors' graves, and they celebrate with food, games, music, and dancing. While Obon is a time of remembering the dead, people do so with a spirit of celebration, and Obon is a happy festival. Chavez says, "It's hard not to agree that Obon is a beautiful tradition. It brings family together from all over the nation and further unites them with siblings, cousins, parents, grandparents, great grandparents and all those before them." At the end of the festival, families set their lanterns afloat to guide the family spirits back to the spirit world.

Amy Chavez, "Five Things You Need to Know About Obon—One of Japan's Biggest Holidays," *RocketNews24* (blog), August 8, 2015. http://en.rocketnews24.com.

[ball-shaped snack usually filled with octopus] and fried noodles. Many of the food stands have their own unique specialty, and there is even a cotton candy stand!" She also describes some of the festival games: "One particularly popular is the scooping goldfish game. You take a scoop with thin paper and dip it in the shallow water in hopes to catch a goldfish. Sometimes the paper rips, though so you won't always be lucky! If you do catch one, it's completely fine to take [it] home with you for your own aquarium!"[72]

Some festivals feature hours-long parades, with groups of dancers—both young and old—in traditional costumes performing for the crowds that gather to watch. Tokyo resident Susan

Dalzell describes the magic and beauty of one such parade at the Tanabata festival, a festival based on a romantic Chinese legend:

> Kimono-clad dancers nimbly parade by, performing traditional dances as loudspeakers blare songs in Japanese. . . . Older women in slim, pink kimonos, their simple hand motions, precise; their hops, dainty. Men in blue pajama-esque robes, with hot pink sashes tied to their backs; each man enthusiastically chopping his hands into the air. Small girls and boys, each kimono brighter than his or her neighbor, tender flowers swaying in the wind.[73]

The most popular of all Japan's festivals are those that celebrate the New Year. The New Year is celebrated from the first to the third of January. Families gather, and most businesses close to mark this occasion. It is customary to clean and decorate the house and to enjoy a number of traditional Japanese dishes such as *ozoni* soup. New Year's celebrations also include a family visit to a shrine or temple, where it is traditional to pray for a happy and healthy year. Tokyo's Meiji Shrine is so popular that it is visited by millions of people during New Year's celebrations. For many young people though, the best part of the New Year's festival is not a visit to the shrine, but the tradition where adults give their children and other young relatives gifts of cash. These gifts are called *otoshidama*, and they vary by age, with older children usually receiving more money. Young people are usually free to spend this money on whatever they want. Yumi Nakata remembers receiving *otoshidama* as a child. "I remember the excitement and joy that I felt as a kid," she says. "I could buy manga, [stationery] and some clothes. So new year was my favorite time of a year."[74]

Festivals for Young People

While young people usually take part in all of Japan's festivals, there are some that are specifically focused on them. Kodomo no Hi, or Children's Day, is May 5, and it celebrates the happiness and health of children. Families fly banners in the shape of carp fish outside their homes. The carp symbolizes strength and determination, which is what families want for their children.

Another common tradition on this day is to display samurai warrior figurines and helmets. A networking group for English-speaking families in Tokyo explains this tradition:

> It's also still very common for families with sons to display a *kintaro* doll and/or a *kabuto* helmet (traditional samurai style helmet), both of which represent a strong, healthy boy. You've probably seen very ornate displays of these objects in department stores and shops like Toys 'R' Us in the run up to the day. A lot of families also still pass down the displays from generation to generation.[75]

On Children's Day, young people get the day off school. They also get to enjoy special desserts such as *kashiwa mochi*, which are sticky rice cakes wrapped in oak leaves, and there are often special community events specifically for young people.

Coming of Age day is in January. This festival celebrates those young people who are turning twenty years old, Japan's official

Young women take a selfie during Coming of Age Day, a festival that celebrates youths who are turning twenty years old, Japan's official age of adulthood.

age of adulthood. Twenty-year-olds are allowed to vote, drink, smoke, and marry without permission from their parents. At ceremonies for Coming of Age Day, which are usually held at the local city hall, women traditionally wear kimonos and men wear suits. Many women spend a lot of money on this celebration, buying expensive kimonos and visiting beauty salons to have their hair and makeup done. For most young people, an important part of the day is when they attend their local shrine with family. At the shrine they pray for health and success in their role as adults. After the ceremony and shrine visit, there is usually a party with family members, lots of photos, and finally, a visit to a bar, since twenty is the legal drinking age in Japan.

As Coming of Age Day celebrations illustrate, religion is a part of life for most Japanese youth. On this day, young people celebrate adulthood by dressing up and attending parties, yet for most, the day is not complete without a trip to the local shrine. Other special events such as funerals or holidays such as New Year's are also tied to religion. Likewise, Japanese young people often include religious rituals in their everyday lives—for example, visiting a shrine to wish for good luck on an exam. Overall, religion is an integral part of life for Japanese young people.

SOURCE NOTES

Chapter One: Japan and Its People

1. Yabe Mitsuo, "Trees and Forests, Part of the Cultural Fabric of Japan," *Nipponia*, March 15, 2003. http://web-japan.org.
2. Ben Cowles, "My Experience During the Japan Earthquake One Year Ago," Expeditioner, March 9, 2012. www.theexpeditioner.com.
3. dasza, "The Shibuya Crossing and New Perspectives," *Perpetual Traveler* (blog), April 28, 2013. www.ptraveler.com.
4. Becki, "What Is Tokyo Like? 16 Things I Love About Japan's Capital City," *Borders of Adventure* (blog), 2017. www.bordersofadventure.com.
5. Kei Keiko, comment on Master Blaster, "Drivers' Licenses? More and More Japanese Youths Don't Need No Stinkin' Licenses," *RocketNews24* (blog), May 19, 2014. http://en.rocketnews24.com.
6. Mary Moriarty, "Shinkansen—the Bullet Train," *The Journey of My Feet* (blog), October 5, 2012. https://thejourneyofmyfeet.wordpress.com.
7. Becky Osawa, "7 Things I Will ALWAYS MISS About Living in Japan," *Trekking with Becky* (blog), August 2, 2016. www.trekkingwithbecky.com.
8. Quoted in Reiji Yoshida, "Japan Census Report Shows Surge in Elderly Population, Many Living Alone," *Japan Times*, June 29, 2016. www.japantimes.co.jp.
9. Grace Buchele Mineta, "9 Things Hated About Living in Tokyo," *Texan in Tokyo* (blog), March 12, 2015. http://howibecametexan.com.
10. Kosuke Furui, "Lower Voting Age Leaves Many Wondering 'Where's Japan's Bernie?,'" Reuters, July 1, 2016. www.reuters.com.

Chapter Two: Home and Family

11. Quoted in CNN, "Tight Squeeze: The Secrets Behind Japan's Coolest Micro Homes," October 17, 2016. www.cnn.com.
12. John Spacey, "What You Need to Know About Futons in Japan," Japan Talk, July 4, 2012. www.japan-talk.com.
13. Quoted in Mary Jordan and Kevin Sullivan, "Japanese Have Little Elbow Room," *Washington Post*, July 29, 1999. www.washingtonpost.com.
14. Quoted in Julie Makinen, "As Japan's Population Shrinks, Bears and Boars Roam Where Schools and Shrines Once Thrived," *Los Angeles Times*, July 10, 2016. www.latimes.com.
15. *Sukiya Living Magazine*, "The Japanese Bath." www.rothteien.com.
16. *Sukiya Living Magazine*, "The Japanese Bath."
17. Becky Osawa, "Growing Up Female in Japan," *Trekking with Becky* (blog), August 3, 2015. www.trekkingwithbecky.com.
18. Mineta, "9 Things Hated About Living in Tokyo."
19. Kaori Shoji, "Where Did All the Japanese Fathers Go?," *Japan Times*, March 23, 2015. www.japantimes.co.jp.
20. Quoted in Sally Herships, "Japan's Population Is Plunging, So Where Are the Babies?," Marketplace, April 20, 2016. www.marketplace.org.
21. Ministry of Health, Labour and Welfare, *Service Guide*, 2015. www.mhlw.go.jp.
22. Quoted in Herships, "Japan's Population Is Plunging, So Where Are the Babies?"
23. Quoted in Herships, "Japan's Population Is Plunging, So Where Are the Babies?"
24. Christine Gross-Loh, "Have American Parents Got It All Backwards?," *Huffington Post*, January 23, 2014. www.huffingtonpost.com.
25. Osawa, "7 Things I Will ALWAYS MISS About Living in Japan."
26. Quoted in Editorial Staff, "The Punctual Japanese," *Hiragana Times*, February 2012. www.hiraganatimes.com.

Chapter Three: Education and Work

27. Candela Guo, "The Busy Life of a Student Studying in Japan," Greenheart Travel, 2013. https://greenhearttravel.org.

28. Karen Ma, "What Is It like Growing Up in Japan?," Quora, August 5, 2014. www.quora.com.
29. Grace Zhang, "What Is It like Growing Up in Japan?," Quora, December 1, 2015. www.quora.com.
30. Quoted in Rebecca Wright, "Japan's Worst Day for Teen Suicides," CNN, September 1, 2015. www.cnn.com.
31. Michael Richey, "20 Differences Between Japanese and Western Schools," *Tofugu* (blog), August 26, 2015. www.tofugu.com.
32. Chico Harlan, "On Japan's School Lunch Menu: A Healthy Meal, Made from Scratch," *Washington Post*, January 26, 2013. www.washingtonpost.com.
33. Quoted in Owen Phillips, "Without Janitors, Students Are in Charge of Keeping School Shipshape," NPR, April 4, 2015. www.npr.org.
34. Kylie Igarashi, comment on Quora, "How Do Japanese Students Feel About the Cleaning Their Own School Rooms and Toilets?," May 3, 2016. www.quora.com.
35. Kylie Igarashi, comment on Quora, "How Do Japanese Students Feel About the Cleaning Their Own School Rooms and Toilets?"
36. Yoshio Sugimoto, *An Introduction to Japanese Society*. Port Melbourne, Australia: Cambridge University Press, 2014, p. 137.
37. Richey, "20 Differences Between Japanese and Western Schools."
38. Louise George Kittaka, "Juku: An Unnecessary Evil or Vital Steppingstone to Success?," *Japan Times*, March 5, 2013. www.japantimes.co.jp.
39. Quoted in Mitsuru Obe, "Japan Rethinks Higher Education in Skills Push," *Wall Street Journal*, August 2, 2015. www.wsj.com.
40. Quoted in Kirk Spitzer, "Young Japanese Job Prospects and Outlook Are Bleak," *USA Today*, September 7, 2014. www.usatoday.com.
41. Quoted in Martin Fackler, "In Japan, Young Face Generational Roadblocks," *New York Times*, January 27, 2011. www.nytimes.com.

42. Quoted in Fackler, "In Japan, Young Face Generational Roadblocks."
43. Quoted in Spitzer, "Young Japanese Job Prospects and Outlook Are Bleak."
44. Quoted in Tomohiro Osaki, "Japan's Low-Earning Adults Find It Hard to Leave Home, Marry," *Japan Times*, May 14, 2015. www.japantimes.co.jp.
45. Quoted in Osaki, "Japan's Low-Earning Adults Find It Hard to Leave Home, Marry."

Chapter Four: Social Life

46. Micah Nathan, "A Female-Fronted Japanese Metal Band Just Took Over Colbert, and They Won't Stop There," *Vanity Fair*, April 8, 2016. www.vanityfair.com.
47. Miyuki E., comment on Yahoo!, "Hows Teen Age Life in Japan??," 2007. https://answers.yahoo.com.
48. Joanne G. Yoshida, "Junior High School in Japan—a Primer for Parents Part II," Japan Visitor, 2017. www.japanvisitor.com.
49. kurisupisu, comment on Japan Today, "What Do You Think of the Quality of School Education in Japan? If You Have a Child at School, Are You Happy with That School?," September 17, 2016. www.japantoday.com.
50. Marie Hayashi Strand, "Introduce Yourself," Global Komaba, January 27, 2015. www.globalkomaba.c.u-tokyo.ac.jp.
51. Quoted in Harumi Ozawa, "'Conformist Society' Pushing Net Addiction Among Japan's Youths," *Japan Times*, February 11, 2015. www.japantimes.co.jp.
52. Quoted in Kristie Wong, "Japan's Social Media Landscape in 2016," *freshtrax* (blog), January 26, 2016. http://blog.btrax.com.
53. Ryan Broderick, "Meet Japan's Most Viral Teenager," BuzzFeed News, March 11, 2016. www.buzzfeed.com.
54. Manami Okazaki and Geoff Johnson, *Kawaii! Japan's Culture of Cuteness*. Munich: Prestel, 2013, p. 13.
55. Okazaki and Johnson, *Kawaii!*, p. 8.
56. *wired2theworld* (blog), "Tokyo's Harajuku Girls and Rockabilly Boys," May 24, 2011. www.wired2theworld.com.

57. *Kansai Scene*, "Confess Your Love!," February 4, 2016. www.kansaiscene.com.
58. Mami Suzuki, "Kokuhaku: Japan's 'Love Confessing' Culture," *Tofugu* (blog), October 23, 2013. www.tofugu.com.
59. Quoted in Abigail Haworth, "Why Have Young People in Japan Stopped Having Sex?," *Guardian* (Manchester), October 20, 2013. www.theguardian.com.
60. Quoted in Nick Whigham, "Around 1 Million Japanese Lock Themselves in Bedrooms and Will Not Come Out," News.com.au, July 13, 2015. www.news.com.au.
61. Shirley S. Wang, "The Fight to Save Japan's Young Shut-Ins," *Wall Street Journal*, January 26, 2015. www.wsj.com.
62. Lorna Petty, comment on Elena Cresci, "What's It like Being LGBT Around the World?," *Guardian* (Manchester), May 16, 2014. www.theguardian.com.
63. Yumi Nakata, "Growing Up as a Hafu in Japan," *GaijinPot* (blog), August 23, 2014. https://blog.gaijinpot.com.
64. Nakata, "Growing Up as a Hafu in Japan."

Chapter Five: Religion

65. Quoted in Rachel Martin, "Buddhism Is Waning in Japan," NPR, November 22, 2015. www.npr.org.
66. Alan Wiren, "Japanese Funerals: Sunset in the Rising Sun," Japan Visitor, 2017. www.japanvisitor.com.
67. Wiren, "Japanese Funerals."
68. Quoted in Naomi Gingold, "Japan Isn't Especially Religious, but There's Still Plenty of Religion," PRI, July 1, 2015. www.pri.org.
69. Chris Betros, "How Religious Are Japanese People?," *Japan Today*, October 27, 2013. www.japantoday.com.
70. Michael Holtz, "In 'Non-Religious' Japan, the Shrine Can Still Exert a Pull," *Christian Science Monitor*, September 6, 2015. www.csmonitor.com.
71. Verity Lane, "Omamori: Protecting Yourself in Little Ways," *Tofugu* (blog), June 25, 2014. www.tofugu.com.
72. Ayumi, "Summer Festivals in Japan," *Tokyo Treat* (blog), August 17, 2015. https://tokyotreat.com.

73. Susan Dalzell, “Finding Magic in the Mystery,” *Susan Dalzell* (blog), August 14, 2014. https://susandalzell.com.
74. Yumi Nakata, “Otoshidama for New Year,” Yumi to Lesson, December 29, 2010. www.yumitolesson.com.
75. Tokyo Mothers Group, “Children’s Day in Japan,” Savvy Tokyo, May 5, 2014. http://savvytokyo.com.

FOR FURTHER RESEARCH

Books

Charlotte Anderson, *The Little Book of Japan*. Tokyo: Tuttle, 2013.

Kira Freed, *Surviving the 2011 Japanese Earthquake and Tsunami*. New York: Rosen, 2016.

Keisuke Matsui, *Geography of Religion in Japan: Religious Space, Landscape and Behavior*. Tokyo: Springer, 2014.

Manami Okazaki and Geoff Johnson, *Kawaii! Japan's Culture of Cuteness*. Munich: Prestel, 2013.

Elise K. Tipton, *Modern Japan: A Social and Political History*. New York: Routledge, 2016.

Internet Sources

Matthew Coslett, "Japan: The Most Religious Atheist Country," *GaijinPot* (blog), February 8, 2015. https://blog.gaijinpot.com/japan-religious-atheist-country/.

Louise George Kittaka, "Juku: An Unnecessary Evil or Vital Steppingstone to Success?," *Japan Times*, March 5, 2013. www.japantimes.co.jp/community/2013/03/05/issues/juku-an-unnecessary-evil-or-vital-steppingstone-to-success/#.WEB9P-YrJPY.

Julie Makinen, "As Japan's Population Shrinks, Bears and Boars Roam Where Schools and Shrines Once Thrived," *Los Angeles Times*, July 10, 2016. www.latimes.com/world/asia/la-fg-japan-population-snap-story.html.

Michael Richey, "20 Differences Between Japanese and Western Schools," *Tofugu* (blog), August 26, 2015. www.tofugu.com/japan/japanese-schools-vs-american-schools.

Kaori Shoji, "Where Did All the Japanese Fathers Go?," *Japan Times*, March 23, 2015. www.japantimes.co.jp/life/2015/03/23/language/japanese-fathers-go/#.WCtz_PorJPY.

Kirk Spitzer, "Young Japanese Job Prospects and Outlook Are Bleak," *USA Today*, September 7, 2014. www.usatoday.com/story/news/world/2014/09/07/japan-young-outlook-bleak/14964463.

Shirley S. Wang, "The Fight to Save Japan's Young Shut-Ins," *Wall Street Journal*, January 26, 2015. www.wsj.com/articles/the-fight-to-save-japans-young-shut-ins-1422292138.

Rebecca Wright, "Japan's Worst Day for Teen Suicides," CNN, September 1, 2015. www.cnn.com/2015/09/01/asia/japan-teen-suicides.

Websites

The *Japan Times* (www.japantimes.co.jp). The website of Japan's oldest English-language newspaper publishes articles about many aspects of Japanese life.

Kids Web Japan (http://web-japan.org). This website, sponsored by Japan's Ministry of Foreign Affairs, provides information about Japanese culture, history, technology, schools, and a variety of other topics.

INDEX

Note: Boldface page numbers indicate illustrations.

PICTURE CREDITS

Cover: Associated Press

6: Maury Aaseng (map)

6: Shutterstock.com/Patrice6000 (flag)

7: iStockphoto/pixelfit (top)

7: Thinkstock Images/iStock: (second, third, and fourth)

9: iStockphoto/Pawel Gaul

12: iStockphoto/Electra-K-Vasileiadou

16: Associated Press

22: Chad Ehlers Stock Connection Worldwide/Newscom

27: iStockphoto/praetorianphoto

29: Ton Koene/VWPics/Newscom

35: iStockphoto/xavierarnau

38: Associated Press

42: iStockphoto/Kobbydagan

45: Associated Press

49: Gili Yaari/Zuma Press/Newscom

53: Associated Press

59: iStockphoto.com/Goddard Photography

61: Associated Press

64: Hitoshi Yamada/NurPhoto/SIPA USA/Newscom

ABOUT THE AUTHOR

Andrea C. Nakaya, a native of New Zealand, holds a BA in English and an MA in communications from San Diego State University. She has written and edited more than forty books on current issues. She currently lives in Encinitas, California, with her husband and their two children, Natalie and Shane.